Praise for Chris Bailey and
Forecast: Pretty Bleak

"I grew up in Southwest Saskatchewan, about as far from a big body of water as you can get, yet these poems by a writer 'baptized by sea' speak in the voices of my prairie ancestors, rough and colourful and true. Few in this country write so eloquently and lyrically about the lives of working people. Chris Bailey throws his net of wonders from his father's boat and pulls in all the tragedy and humour a life can hold. Often what gets caught are wise lines that break the heart: 'Maybe it's best to learn the hard things young / and never forget.' I won't forget this book."

—Lorna Crozier, author of *After That*

"Chris Bailey's plainspoken, clear-eyed poems transmit the perils of 'Existence / carved from sandstone, baptized by sea' with an eloquence that remains rooted in both its vernacular music and the harsh demands of work. Scrupulously spare yet deeply moving, they recall the work of Alden Nowlan. This is essential reading."

—Don McKay, author of *Lurch*

"Clear-eyed and unflinching, but also compassionate, Chris Bailey writes of the realities of commercial fishing in contemporary PEI, 'of blood and sea.' His poems showcase a storyteller's gift for character and narrative tension, attending to the desires, loves, and fears that accompany us through our days."

—Annick MacAskill, author of *Votive*

Praise for Chris Bailey and
What Your Hands Have Done

"Bailey's work explores questions of identity: family and roots—mostly working class—character portraits and poems of romance. There's much to admire in these short, clean stanzas and the landscape that shines through behind them—its pine trees and cold rain, its lobster and herring gear, its dark sky and restless ocean."
—Joseph Millar, author of *Shine*

"[Bailey] often relies on a lean vernacular to portray that grueling way of life and those he shares it with."
—Barbara Carey, *Toronto Star*

"Chris Bailey canvases easily—adroitly—that difficult, East Coast world of hard-scrabble, hard-luck ports and hard-living, hard-drinking fishers, the epicureans of cynicism and the aesthetes of brutalism. Think E.J. Pratt meets Charles Bukowski."
—George Elliott Clarke, author of *J'Accuse...!: (Poem Versus Silence)*

"Bailey's voice here is all authentic."   —*Atlantic Books Today*

"This is no quaint voice from the Land of Anne. Suffused with our era's geist and angst, which have penetrated to the rural periphery, Bailey is a sharp-eyed, clarion-voiced witness in his crow's nest."   —Richard Lemm, author of *Jeopardy*

"While the poems in this collection are rooted in East Coast life, their themes reveal themselves in a darker universality that concerns common patterns of masculine existence."
—A.W. French, *Hamilton Review of Books*

FORECAST: PRETTY BLEAK

Poems

CHRIS BAILEY

McClelland & Stewart

McClelland & Stewart and colophon are registered trademarks of Penguin Random House Canada Limited.

Published simultaneously in the United States of America.

The authorized representative in the EU for product safety and compliance is Penguin Random House Ireland, Morrison Chambers, 32 Nassau Street, Dublin D02 YH68, Ireland. https://eu-contact.penguin.ie

Library and Archives Canada Cataloguing in Publication
Title: Forecast: pretty bleak : poems / Chris Bailey.
Names: Bailey, Chris, 1990- author
Identifiers: Canadiana (print) 20240422082 | Canadiana (ebook) 20240422090 |
    ISBN 9780771020490 (softcover) | ISBN 9780771020506 (EPUB)
Subjects: LCGFT: Poetry.
Classification: LCC PS8603.A44325 F67 2025 | DDC C811/.6—dc23

Cover design by Andrew Roberts
Cover art: SKC / Stocksy
Typeset in Legacy by Sean Tai
Printed in Canada

McClelland & Stewart,
a division of Penguin Random House Canada Limited,
320 Front Street West, Suite 1400,
Toronto Ontario, M5V 3B6, Canada
penguinrandomhouse.ca

1 2 3 4 5   29 28 27 26 25

Penguin
Random House
McCLELLAND & STEWART

CONTENTS

For those whose outlook ain't too shit-hot.
Things may not improve, but the weather might,
if you're lucky enough for time to wait.

FORECAST:
PRETTY BLEAK

WHERE MOST
ACCIDENTS HAPPEN

ALL THIS IS

Each morning makes promises that can't be kept,
instead hands over the same length of being you been
spliced in from the jump. Another day in life given
without asking. Office work foreign as tundra,

some desert named like warning or whatever stirs
in now-dead stars tacked up before your grandfather
was a thought or shot in the dark, allows them to shine
bright in the mind of the child you know will move

into rubber boots and oil gear smooth as sea at slack
tide with no wind to speak of. Keep to yourself
your uncle's words: *Survival, that's all this is.*
A desire to not have the last taste on your tongue
be this brine you hauled part-dollars and sanity

and four walls from. Your father showed you
to frame traps, rig parlours, tie proper knots.
The ocean repeats itself like family, like history,
ports along a shore. Coiling backline, your father said,

We won't change the world doing what we do.
And when we're gone who cares for us?
Some say they do, and they do. But give it a week,
a month. And it's like we never were.

STARTING OUT

The man your father first fished for,
his body went to science.

You could shit a gold brick,
your father says, *and that rotten prick*
could still find something wrong, and fuck you.

Hard days on hard water and your father
told to haul gear that wasn't theirs for his
fucking paycheque. Evenings they loaded

the truckbed with buoys given the Green River,
your father and the eel skinner headed with them
wherever, some plot of cold earth to be burnt.

I didn't even know he had a heart till the doctor
split his chest and found it. Surprised us all.

Your father's eyes were pointed to Thompson then,
nickel mines. What they filled with was seawater,
mackerel blood. The scales of herring used as bait.

YOUR MOTHER CALLS

An uncle is in the Dying Room with cancer
in his spine. One last ambulance ride down along
the southside to make final visits easier for his wife.

It's too bad, you say. *It's too bad about all that.*

Well it's done now. There's nothing a person can do.

Then she asks how you're doing. You speak in forecast:
rain and lightning along escarpment ridge. Wind roaring
from the north before hauling around west,
and the temperature is falling.

You drew blood from your fist that kissed
a wall with a crack. Poor club of bone, the wall
of cement. Another broke rope from oak trap
caught on rock, snared on some lost anchor
left from when herring shoals still rolled in.

Moved cross-country. Took residence in one city
where you were an organ of the wrong blood type
in a body on the table. Another with words carved
in the sidewalk, art for sale the second Friday
evening of every month on James Street.

Lobster traps are décor here. Fishing is for sport.
You went without wood slabs to stack and cast
a tarp across to show your love. Only words,
roves of time rasped thin between lobster seasons
and mackerel runs. Scraps not enough to feed off.

PREPARING TO LEAVE

My love, I walk floors I've swept, washed,
swept and washed again and again
to satisfy my hands, my mind. They say
idle hands are what the devil prefers, but consider
the mind idling on its own.

I look out my window, south, where you live and avoid
the east and the work waiting there. Existence
carved from sandstone, baptized by sea. Life breathed
into being by nor'east winds that knot trawls,
keep boats bound to their berths.

Tonight, I walk the neighbourhood we share.
The street smells of fresh laundry. A couple stops me
for directions to James Street and the man asks to hack
a dart and I apologize for how I look, for this old coat,
this load on my shoulders that stoops me just so.

WAITING FOR A PLANE

At a Pearson Airport bar, the man next to me talks
working forestry in Grand Prairie, felling heads,
shows off the Caterpillar cable skidder used
to load trucks with logs. His dad wants him
home in Fredericton to stay: *He says,*
You'll just spend your money on hookers out there.

I tell him my father's the opposite. Thinks
I should get out more: *You work your life*
away and what you get at the end is same
as someone prone to lazation, young fella.

An hour drank away as people arrive, pay,
depart for entire lives beyond gates
I don't have the bravery to stick my head in.
No happiness where I'm to, nothing more fierce
than whore eggs piercing gloves, the bilge stink

pissed out the portside and blown back.
This man's off to PEI for a wedding, and asks
what Ontario folk think of the Island,
of New Brunswick, of Cape Breton.

It's all Newfoundland to them, man.

THE HEART IS A KNOT

My father says, *And the heart is the softest part*
of the hardwood. It's so close to rot,

as we tack oak lath into the arses of traps, no
light tap, no gentle touch in this building
drug home from the harbour on creosote skids,
hauled with thick chains, its cement footprint
left cratered at the lake. Find nailhead
with hammer's face, let your hand be heavy

like the weight of February cold, its wind
with so much north in it, shores shift:
the harbour mouth fills, chokes with sand
each year. The jut of land between North Lake
and East Point gone like good oak for traps

gone for the floors of large houses that sit
empty ¾ of the year. Part-time residents
who want full-time say over taxes,
pavement, over windmills that churn
Island air their lungs seldom breathe.

My father says, *You'd get junks of cod*
come up in the gear like this.
How far apart he holds his hands.

And now. He stops, shakes his head.
Points to the laths I've driven in.

THE USES FOR ROPE

At crow piss this morning
your father spliced eyes into
lengths of line for buoy extensions.

You should've woke me, you say,
I would've helped.

> *Well, you'd have to learn first.*
> *It don't take much. I'll teach you.*

You think of the uses
for rope fishermen have.
Stern to cleat, and the bowline

hitched. Trawl gear, tiedowns.
An end stretched across
crossbeams, through oakdust
choked workshops, lit by a lone
trouble light, the skeletal frames of traps to witness.

APRIL 21

Yesterday the last snowfall of the season.
Bukowski said love is a fog that burns up
at first light of day, but what does he know?
Love is late winter, snow come on harder
than expected, lasts longer than it should
on nor'west winds off the Gulf. A slow turn
to water that can't be grasped. And tomorrow
grass will try to grow and be greener
in the hollows of spruce and poplar.

DIRT

What little there is left of me. Dirt
on Tom's big hands that lugged seismic cable, bucked
hundred-pound potato bags in grade school.
Lit cigarettes on hard days, split lips, broke noses.
He blames the clay and pine needles not on the wind
or trees or fields, but on Will's tarp he leant Tom for winter.
It's dirtier than a new shit stain in old underwear, Tom says,
this filth of our lives, our occupation. After a spring
spent unloading crab boats, I'd stuff my clothes into
the incinerator, turn their stink to ash, scratch at scabs
on 12-year-old forearms chewed up by crab juice.
After shaking nets for a season, you can shower and shower
and months later find herring spawn hiding. A woman I loved who
slept with someone else after we first said *I love you.*
Rust and oil cover Tom's hands now as he lies on the floor,
reaches below with a wrench to the engine, an attempt
to get the electric clutch to turn, but it's seized up.

CUTTING BAIT

Your father calls Eastern Cold Storage in Souris
to let Andre know: five boxes today, sixteen total.
Mackerel froze in forty-pound blocks caught last July,
last August. Awash in seawater, ice shovelled
to slurry blood and shit, keep the fish fresh for freezing.

Forget the bandsaw's dull blade, its teeth squared off
from last year. Why change this? The small marvel
of your brother and father preferring to slide the block
through slow, chance the frost and forgot hooks
that want to jump the blade, make a fuck of a time.
This season's first argument over the guide, its setting
to get twenty-four blocks a box, settles low-tide predictable:
three and a quarter inches.

Remember: your father thinks himself right,
and your brother thinks *him*self right,
while you are paid partly to be wrong. Breathe.
Look: spring sky cleaned of clouds. Moon
faded, lingering in blue.

THE BOAT HAULER

Ryan backs down the 300-foot gravel lane
to *Grampy's Boat* in its building built the summer
of '88, your brother Peter going or gone
down to St. Columba and your father's lodestar
heart, diligent-sharp, drove him to frame and strap,
instead of simply slapping moonshine to this wound.
The same drive placed him here pacing and waiting
45 minutes before the hauler turned north on Elmira.
He sledgehammers blocking, quick movements
of a practiced carcass, creosote clatters like old bones
on cement floor, split and oil-stained. There's a conversation
can't quite be heard over engine-rumble, winch-whine.
Your father speaking, then the hauler: *Arnold,*
all the young fellas have around here is crushed dreams.

SHINGLING A ROOF IN INTERMITTENT SNOW

You said PEI looks like paradise
in your folks' giftshop photos. But, darling,
a photo can't catch the cold quite like a hand,
ungloved and gripping a hammer, can it?

Count the hours between hurry up and wait
and you'll be counting till after my brothers
make an Elliott's run, bait on their tailgates
waiting to thaw under what's meant to be the sun.
Up here, I try to see what could be beautiful:

> snowmelt in malnourished grass,
> pressure-treated spruce
> to keep swelling out the walls,
> the chalk horizon, the slate
> clouds, how Abel said,

> *Look: there's a difference*
> *between scratchin your arse*
> *and tearin it all to pieces.*

SETTING DAY

Throw on oil gear not for safety but to stave off
cold that turns to sweat when you toss traps,
buoys. Pull and kick rope where it won't catch.
Shout numbers to the cabin, face the bow,
shout *loud*, or else all will hear is needle-teethed
surf, nor'east wind that don't give a fuck about you.

Pack the second load on, the third. Bottom row
on edge, snood toward stern, ballast starboard.
Next row on their flat, five high like that with rope
coiled under traps, trawls taking the shape
of eels striving to seethe from the sea to sky.

When running the gear off watch for backline
at your feet. Remember the knife Tom
taped to the boom. If time comes you're caught,
cut the line waterside, unless you wish for burial
below this great unfathomable thing
that don't want you, save for when it wants entirely.

WHAT I CAN TALK ABOUT

Been lobster fishing and the catches, fuck.
I can't talk about them, what goes across the scales, no.
You want to hear of gannets plugging, or the tug
of the tide when the boat steams too fast to gaff easy,
then, yeah. But landings are double-oh-7, and whisky is cheap.
What I can talk about is the soreness of cracked hands
come Sunday when tap water runs over them, cold
air off the water. Frost in nostril hair. The woman I love
half a country, a whole life away, in the company of lesser men,
of better men. Wasting small hours with the vacant-hearted
and soft-handed who don't know the grounds to fish.

HOME IS

where most accidents happen. Do a headcount
of you, your brothers and your sisters

to confirm. Where you dreamt dreams
of a landlocked life beyond your trimless window
with its pilled orange blanket-curtain, years after

your first hurricane where you stood out with Brandon
in the meteorologic baptism of Juan's waters, filling buckets
for toilet flushing by low kerosene lantern glow. The only

photo on the wall then was Gretzky and his father,
given to your father when he bought his first brand new rig,
a Ranger, after the wallpaper went up. Home is the name

of the place you outgrew, the chitin casing you thrashed
your fresh skin against that last growth spurt
when the tide surged level with the wharf.

Home is where, like a rockstar, you're most apt to die
on the shitter. The safest place to hang your head.

ABEL

Abel tells you about the time he was 3 and caught crabs
from kids in a sandbox. His mother plucking every eyelash.
He reads fantasy, and Hunter S. Thompson. When he reads
he wants to be taken away from this seaside town,
this waterfront province with more memory than new rope.
Always good for a laugh, he says to your nephew Zach:

I'd take your mother out the Glen Road and tell her
you're only young once so here's a smash
of rum and you're up next on this toke. I was 17.
I'm not saying I was trying to see her naked, but
I like big titties. And she had big ones.

The three of you opening bait bags. Washed-out
landscape of cold PEI spring. What will be
green waits to grow and birds wait for warmth to sing.

Now, look, bud: I'm not sayin I'm the manliest of men.
I'm not gonna get grease on my hands or change a tire.
But I go into Charlottetown? It's like I stepped
straight out the fuckin woods.

RESILIENCE

I

My love, on the boat my father said, *Time.*
There is always time. But what gets done
with it is another matter.

I was running a trawl up the washboard
on the Gulf of St. Lawrence, offshore,
130 feet deep. Edged gear headed south,
the inside ground. 6 trips, 24 trawls gone
beaching as though the wind won't blow
north or east. There is a clock in my head,
and Kyle and I are talking, coffee in hand,
Souris Harbour before us, parked in his old Yaris.

We go on about the day, what this is all for.
His goal's to get the mortgage paid, time with his kids
all growing like bad habits come Saturday night.
Both his folks passed young, and he wants
nothing more than family, to provide. Security.

Do you remember outside that bar in Toronto?
When you said to me, *I'm late*
and instead of trying to run or placate I said,
Whatever you want to do, I'm here

and the winter was lifting in Toronto then.
Snow melting in sunshine, freezing come night.
Buds in the trees. You point and say,
Look, Chris. Nature is resilient. Put another
cigarette in your mouth for me to light.

II

There are life vests we are to wear but few
have took to them, $400 fine be fucked.
My father says, *They're not to save your life*
but to make sure there's a body to bury.
A weak requisite to hang them off your carcass
when six feet or less from the wharf's edge. A hardhat
if a hoist is at work, boots with steel toes.
When my father first started at this, he wore blue gloves,
canvas, and wrung them out by closing a fist.

I'm sick of these sunrises, darling. Each one paid
for by a day feeling without end. But today was something:
red red *red* horizon and Cape Breton rising from slurry
of blood and sea. A rainbow gradient, indigo upstairs.
I never seen green in the sky but been told
it holds over Kentucky when a twister is coming.

Here a twister don't mean wind or fate, but a heart
worked itself silent. To take a twister
is to shorten Helwig's ten feet between yourself and death.
It happens to the old, the young, and is a grace given
to those who twist in seats and load a shotgun
into their mouths or cast a line across a workshop rafter
though everyone will know the truth of who set you to twist.

A fella at the harbour tried
to do himself in with a flaregun.
Spent three months unable to talk
and now words spill out
his mouth like the shits,
him saying to Zach: *Stay away from that*
one—if she's anything like her mother,
there's more loose skin down there
than you know what to do with.

A young man drowned downshore today.
Water so calm, they say *cam*, the word itself gone
piss-flat like glass. He went to take in a chafer
and caught a wave. All they found: His gloves.
His oil coat. A new-this-season pair of rubber boots.
I am told his father meant to shorten the line
last night, but that's talk in a place where all there is
is work and talk and   there was the man

who asked where my father was to one afternoon
as I arranged things on deck to dry and avoid gullshit.
Him sober for a day, and then, seeing things
how they were, handled matters in a manner I feared
my father would steer himself, lobster traps stacked
against a plywood door, the creak of backline
out in the building where he built our lives
my whole life. All that is inevitable:
death, taxes, Mondays are bait days.

THE WATER GOD

Fished sixty full years for bragging rights.
Got Peter Stewart's tuna rods for a song,

or a bit of blood and a blessing. His heart
quit more than once, but he keeps on. You know

only one thing so long you become it, so why be shy
of going out alone? His shoal of children gone on

beyond the bell buoy's toll, the blinkered lighthouse
on the Point that holds his field-glass eyes he puts to shore,

a witness to each inevitable sinking. The knowledge
one person's grave can be another's home.

LANDING DAY

Lobster traps get piled five high or stood in drives
to dry, and you get a point and a half of vodka into you,
not letting that bottle suffer none, no, not while
quieting the low screech of your back, the pitch
in your mind saying that's another two months lost
or sold off. Try to gaff hold of your buddy
who got twisted as Christ spiked one-handed to the cross
and wandered your cousins' hallway saying,
Which bedroom's the bathroom?
at 3 in the afternoon. What you do and what you want
to do are not the same thing. Time's tide rips
you off to the Rafter for the Landing Day dance.
Names and faces repeat themselves like a plunge
of gannets while you drift through the queue, while you wait
20 minutes for a bartender to fuck up your order
of whisky and water, for her to not know your name
in a place supposed to be home.

WANTING ON A SUMMER DAY

Streetlights outside your living room blink slow
to life while the sun sinks into skyscrapers.
You roll a joint against a glamour mag
after your daughter's in bed, and we take a blanket
to the backyard, smooth it down in the confines of your life,

nurse beer, exhale lazy smoke toward sky polluted
by city night. Fireflies burn out between
blackened bulbs of unlit Christmas lights
in the trees. So much gone on there's so little left
to say. Even wild rivers flow quiet in familiar

hillsides. Our goodbye: a hug, a kiss on your
neck, your cheek, the corner of your mouth.
We have to be good, you say.
My car pulls onto a night-dark street. Porch light
in your hair, your hand a brief current of waves

and today is grey with swollen clouds. Out my window,
it wants to rain. The skies want to open
and the trees want a drink, and the wind wishes
it could blow cool from the north and smell
like sea. And what is it I want for? And you?

A fisherman who drank, smoked, and watched hockey.
Put cold molasses on fresh biscuits and whose hands
commanded whatever carpentry tool they put to use.
He died before you knew what work or words were.

Old Peter fished charters, kept a notebook for this.
Your grandmother didn't care for the Mexicans, come up
through Montreal putting money down on women,
and when the Baptist pastor came to dinner, Margaret, she said,

Now, Peter, don't be saying Sniffling Jesus this, or
Fuck that over there. He's a man of the cloth!

What's left of him: sepia-toned photos, his bald spot
same as your brother's, your cousin's and nephew's.
The squareness of lobster traps you belong to
come May and June, the spit of time between seasons.

AENEAS

A great-grandfather you never knew,
that your father never knew outside
things gleaned from the internet, dubious
books, a childhood half-remembered
between terse words and dreams of work,

this man all the things you never quite were:
Carpenter. Farmer. Competition-entering
fiddle player that never made it to Boston.
Was a Cheverie, the mailman, that took that ticket.
He did all he could want till that spring morning,

Aeneas to the barn to shoe a horse. One kick,
and a spike burst through his foot. And after?
Blood poisoning, the fever. Him in bed with breaths
akin to puffs of air, less than smoke. That Tuesday
spent dying in the last log house left in Elmira.

AUGUSTUS

Tall with hair thicker than Setting Day fog
or the hands of men before and after him,
who hammer and saw, pull and drag their lives
away to keep the switch on the wall working.

He met his wife in Montreal while he was foreman
in a munition plant, and, let's face it, part fool
like every other man in your family. Word sent
his log house was set fire to, his lumber loaded
on a train as replacement stolen the first time.

What you know: he called you *Skipper*
as a child. Held you gleefully as you handfed
goslings in his kitchen. That Peter was his favourite
till both their ends. That he favoured dark rum.

I wanna talk to my friends who drink the clear stuff
I gotta go to the goddamned graveyard.

LITTLE BITTY

At 12 you learn about death and lobster traps
in the south building. You don't focus on your father
saying, *I'm worth more dead than alive*,
but on instruction: angle that saw, boy. A hammer demands
confidence. Spoke-shave squared posts to save your hands
in spring. You hate to rig them, hate the melted plastic
stink of twine cut so much the hot knife's smoulder
has you give your guts to a snowbank. The good air follows
you back to where your father is, head down, saying
nothing. Alan Jackson on the radio he found at the dump.
This song has everything there is in a life, he says.
This is what I want played at my funeral.
And you wish you were 5 again. That your father
would hold you, kiss your cheek. Place a hand
on your shoulder before wishing you goodnight.

WE TALKED ABOUT THIS

I

A wore building door swings
on corroded hinges. The fire suffers
in the furnace and the paint is 17 years old.

Black doors, white trim. Black woodblock buttons.
Me held in the tractor bucket, me as a child,
to finish up with a brush. This is how we changed

the outside bulbs, then. My father's voice:
Home is a place the door is never shut.

2

In the lane, mud, the burnt black/grey ash stain
left by garbage lit against a shrinking snowbank.
Crows gone. My father runs a nail gun, spikes
rubbers to four boughs a trap on traps he will take
to the harbour alone, until Zach wakes up.
This season: a small disagreement rips a large rift,
but only one person's to lift it. Blame is something
I am made to carry. No other man in my family
has ever done a wrong. *I'm sorry* are words
spoken in dreams, by people on TV shows,
one person bumping into another at a grocery store.

3

On the phone, Steve says some guy from Summerside
was poet laureate of the United States, and the idea
of thriving off-Island seems so far, a spike

in the sky lit like a light I might call *star*, what could be
called *heart*, what I shut my eyes to those nights
filled with windmill thrum on a bitter easterly

bend, the mind perceiving this not as sign, but as pulse
of some prime mover moved only by reprisal
beyond any coloured horizon that surrounds me.

Sons leave home. We've always had to
leave the Island. It's how paradise works.

He gives advice I gave when dealing
with a loved one. How disproportionate
the importance of facts faced again:

It's not for us to say I told you so, but
to help them through what happens after.

4

You'd be loon-foolish to not be nervous
come Setting, all that weight, so much
rope gone over, all in thick fog with a rock
on from the north, and the tide against you.

Those who die tend to spend final hours, final days
doing the mundane: running low on dish soap,
pounding off to internet porn, brushing their teeth
for shorter than dentists recommend. Hearing or saying
something that will never be taken back.

When we go to sink the traps that first day:
nor'west wind, water whitecapping. A man in a kilt
stands on flagstone, plays bagpipes, his song
sounding like a funeral to each boat sailing out the run.

5

My father's hand is crushed
between a trap and hauler claw.
Blood blooms in latex glove.
White slough of dead skin.
The thing about water: it makes blood
appear so much more than it is.

6

A twist in the north wind that's cold and busy
rearranging things on deck, in the cabin, the scramble
of tools and water bottles on a fibreglass floor
that's not always there when you need it, and Tom

with the sooks on: *I bet you fucking William*
has more fucking fish than this, so we haul
back extra for turkeys, return the rest
to wire-bottom traps, parlours stitched shut

when a half-haul'd meet the quota put on
by the buyer: *We're still short thirty workers, Arnold*,
and so tomorrow it's only markets, and the chickenhawk
might get our canners. Another long day promised,

but we will return to a bridge with new pavement.
The excavator up digging by the road staked, painted.
My father built the old bridge in a '70s summer,
fistful of years before Peter was born, a decade before
he passed. Dad has only said it was hot, that he caught
a nine-pound sledge to the side of his head.

Right bang-oh. Then: stars.
Every fucking universe imaginable.

7

A friend calls to confess an affair,
and I listen and say to him:
I would have advised against this.

Birdshit streaks shingles on the house's
south side. Crows pick lobster shells clean
in a garden yet to be tilled. I do not know
enough of the tides to write proper about them,
to call myself captain, to be at the helm
and run two trawls off on edge, to end up greater
than the copper clay rising away from dry fields
as I hear his reasons. I understand him, them.
But how do you feel?

Can a heart be broke clean enough to heal
so smooth you must know where to look
to see where it was broken?

8

I want to tell you things of this place:

My father says something *puts the tag on the toe*
instead of a bow gone on.
Put a pane in that hole, he says
when he wants a truck window rolled up.

To *fill your boots* means go right ahead,
take your fill, that if you got good driving
you're *bootin er right along* that your mickey
is a pint is my point of whisky seeing as I'm east
of Georgetown, so far down east you're headed up
again, and don't let no one tell you different.

How my uncle Michael said of his ailing girlfriend,
I wouldn't have given five cents for her in the winter,
but look. She's doing better. Can't you see?
and of another woman:
She's too mean to buy gas for the saw.

9

When we go to tie up, my uncle Michael sits
on a tank by my father's building with Westie,
Old Bullhead, telling and being told lies
about previous lives, political unravellings,
what they seen on the long drive east.

Thirty-some years ago, Westie says, there was
a big Black fella about seven feet tall,
shoulders on him like this from New York,
and worked for the *mahfia* buying tuna
and said, *That's a nice-looking fish. Can I buy it?*

So what if we reek of blood and sea? The work
that sustains us trailing like a course line
on a Hondex plotter. We get closer and Michael don't
mind, he's retired, and Westie is, too, and he says:

He paid me $18,000, cash. I thought I was rich.
And don't you know I went down to the liquor store,
got a six pack of beer and the next morning
had four left for the hangover.

10

You ask what a gaspereau is, this fish
that's like herring, but not in the eyes
of fishermen. It sounds French, but
who knows where *gaspereau* originates?

Named *alewife* on the Wiki page
for the roundness, paunch little belly
shaped like tavern wives, women brewers,
bartenders back in the day. You say,

Oh my God, the etymology,
and I say I'll have to take some time, rewrite
The Cranewife story and call it *The Alewife.*
           Yes. You have to do that.

II

My father says a buyer is the chickenhawk.
When he was young he nicked a few things
from a farm and was discovered
when the trunk lid was lifted and feathers
rose out, all racket and beak and talon
and shit-stink. I do not know who opened it
or why, or where, but when I'm told this
I picture a shore folding into troubled water,
slashed white by wind, eelgrass bent like June
tourists at the wharf looking for a feed.

My father says to me,
I wouldn't lie to you.

But you've been mistaken.

Yes, that's the word. Mistaken.

Kenny fires three people in one day.
One, his daughter, flips him off, shouts
while stomping up the shingled ramp,
Can you fucking hear me now?

His son peels off his oil pants, lifts them,
a mackerel-scaled flag on the floating dock,
and lets the harbour have them. Open palms
pound a Chevy truck. A howl and he's gone.

Kenny shakes his head, a man whose sounder
is dead, the depth and bottom below him unknown.
He lights joint number whatever for the day, says
to us, *Respect used to be a big word around here.*

13

This morning spent in the shallows, 15 feet
and how red the sandstone cliffs, how clear
the water, the sharpness of stone in bent light
lighting parlours filled with lobster, rock crab

crawled in off sand bottom. Evergreens alongside
a patch of dead trees bleached white by seaspray
and sun. Driftwood standing and yet to fall into
its name. When I see things like this, I long to describe
them to you. Did I forget the gannets diving,

plugging away at bait in water columns?
They plummet 100 klicks an hour, chests puffed
to ease impact against the sudden
embrace of water, to prevent internal damage.

You say, *I heard the word* mackerel *yesterday
and thought of you.*

14

Low catches set teeth on edge, and Will struggles
to fish and be apart from family he built—what he expected
of Kyle last season, what's been expected of Kyle for years.
Will misses his wife, his son. Their newborn the first
first-boy not named after Peter. Will says,
>   *I don't want him stuck in the past.*
>   *I want him to be his own person.*

Will fills me in on harbour ruckus: Kenny and his brother
chirping at wharf workers, and Tommy flying
into them. Kenny pushes Tom with two hands,
tries to lift his fists from his pockets. Tom's big smirk
and Kenny beaks off at Will, mouth like an old bait bag.
Kenny throws a can of Pepsi, says, *I meant that for your head.*

When our father hears this, Tom going aboard Kenny,
crash of pop can against sheet metal siding, he says,
The old man would say a good blast never hurt anyone,
it just might make them think for once.

15

How to safely admit to love at a distance:
obtusely, at angles. Point to things done

or said: a pool deck built with your father,
a slide you hold for your son to slide down.

A half-remembered Barbie book read aloud
to Bonnie's girls growing in Cornwall and you

taking a photo of the Barbie section in a DVD aisle.
Notes sung from your daughter's piano

and played for me in a video facing a wall,
in a hall: a door that is not wholly shut.

16

Hearts are barbed mackerel hooks
that break like so much of life

between stainless steel pipes
held tight by vise grips. They ache

without being broke. A big toe smashed
between a lead weight and fibreglass.

17

Yesterday, weather on the horizon
toward Cape Breton. Sun rising.

Slate-coloured clouds, their camber,
great columns of rain across the Strait.

Tailings spill off, a bit of buoy paint
on an old sneaker from years back.

When I speak of sky I know I say
nothing new. Sometimes you talk

to say nothing, to hear a voice call in response.

18

You speak of your children:

your son wants to walk along this river,
this slow roll of water you describe as
someplace you'd go dump a body.

You want your daughter to know
there's more to a woman's life than what's expected,
what Kyle and Bianca call *pink chores.*

You show me your bedroom layout. Beds for both
kids when scared, say, *I haven't dated anyone*
important since my son was born.

19

At Elliott's I take a photo of the building,
the sign leading to the beach we spent
what passed for childhood—Brandon and me,
our cousins from New Brunswick who brought

their contraband pop in cans and plastic, before
I put my foot to a gas pedal, knelt in crab juice
of a boat's hole, the crew toking and drinking
and asking who owned us.

Inside for nothing stiffer than a bag of chips,
a tank of gas. The worker has her hair tied back,
red headband, tanned skin. She says she's sorry.
We're all out of tens.

That's fine, I say, I'm sure
the fives will add up.

The words *mail the letters* smudged
on the back of her left hand. A time was
she would unload those boats with us,
cause a crabalanche into a pan wanting ice, and

can you picture the sea south of here? The ferry
steaming to the Maggies. Hutt boats gone with washboards
loaded. Smell the air: saltwater and hot sand,
or the copper scent of mud after rain.

20

Wind from the north, and rain,
a white ridge boils along the run. No out,
but waiting to do bait, that anticipatory way
of hurrying up just to wait and wait and wait

and Saturday and that same rain still falls.
My father and I move traps, stack them
on a haywagon. These were meant for Kenny,
but my father says to a Gallant of the man,
He's been a real prick to the grandson, so fuck that.
I'll take them home and burn them first.

Oh, is he now?

A right proper prick, yes.
The only thing missing is the balls.

21

Sometimes what's needed to find
misery is to open your eyes.
An old fisherman said

One mackerel and a litre of water
is all you need to make a real mess.

Other things: Will sits on a pallet
with a broken lath, hacks a cigarette, and says
his wife got mad at the dog for dreaming last night.

Me saying to Zach at the kitchen table,
How cranky are you on a scale of one to go-fuck-yourself?
                    Oh, I'm not too bad.

A welder talks geometry, the hydraulic cylinder,
what it means for the boom's arm with a trap on:
It pivots here, it'll come in to get you.

My father feeds rock eel to two large eagles
atop the sandpile on the run's north side.
Something'll get a fucking bite anyway, he says,

as we hear lobster's left to rot on purpose, insurance
money, you see. Cleaner than arson, trucks
run up west to the hammermill. More dumped

on the Paddy Road, where there used to be a school,
where my father and I cut lumber for firewood,
for the oak lath of lobster traps.

23

You send pictures of yourself, a video,
and say, *I was thinking of you,*
and then we do this together, are together,
and after, and afterwards

a closeness. Intimacy. Is this
how distance is supposed to be?
My eyes shut and I am with you.
Why would I want to open them here?

At Kyle's on Saturdays I bring Schooner
and the sooner we dig into them the better.
I tell Bianca and him that Matt Lieb calls liquor
momma's mean juice
due to how his wife treats him while boozing.

Kyle says, *You hear that, Bonk?*
Sounds like someone around here.
                    Oh, fuck off, Kyle.

Bianca smiles, pours a rum drink after ten-plus
hours working. Kyle was hit by a snowplough
on foot in January, the doctor saying people should
grow old slow, and this did him fast. He calls
Bianca his sugar momma. *She does a lot, man.*
She's working for two now.

25

You are comfort in what passes for life
here. If only school wasn't two years,
if only there wasn't a pandemic. If only
all that is needed is to open a door. Walk out
of my bedroom and into a life together.
Coffee cools on the counter. In the backyard,
a small shed waits to be painted, holds the mower
in need of oil. You take me by the hand, lead me
to tomatoes you potted with your son, your daughter.
Gesture to the lettuce waiting for water.

26

So hot my oil jacket is lost at first crack, jellyfish
and possible skin cancers be damned, and the catch,

Christ, down a hundred pounds and Tom gone on:
Maybe gaspereau ain't as good as we thought.

Yesterday it was the best thing took place since
his boots hit boat floorboards, since his middle son

learned to turn a mackerel reel, to take the bow line
in both hands, half-hitch it to the wharf without instruction.

27

When we land the lobster gear, Brandon and James
show up to help, and Brandon talks like Brandon does:

Guys at work were talking about going to the lake
or the beach without me, so I said,
I'm red seal at giving head. I'll suck your dicks, boys.

Says to Tommy how they used to be so close,
that they used to have tickle fights.
Why are you being so mean, Tom?
Why can't we be like we used to be?
                              You're fucked, Brandon.

Day foggy at first but the sun rose, burnt
it off like bad fuel in a tank and the engine
revved in neutral. Sweat rolls, traps are tossed
and stacked on the wharf and Tommy says to Zach,
Now did you see that ten-pound market?
                              I was gonna ask
                              where you got the small fishpan at.

Brandon sits like our father after we raked
17, 000 pounds of gravel for a floor he won't use
again, laughs and says, *Princess Auto! Don't ya know?*
They're on sale half-off!

28

Striped and silver bodies of mackerel quiver,
shiver their lives away in plastic trays of chutes.
Fall into tanks. Bleed out, breathe in
their own blood till they drown. Nothing like nightmares
till a hook hooks one between the eyes,
catches a pipe, leaves the big half of its face
on the line. An eyeball dangles, the body
trembles like Zach's retriever when thunder rolls.

I see this and think how different a life you lead, have led.
You, this woman who went to her daughter's room
with gentle hands and took from that room a spider,
walked down to the door to set it loose in the yard.
When I think of this it is night. Stars pinned like gloves
to dry from the sky above your house. A warm breeze
in lilac trees. Fireflies flash. You watch this spider vanish
between blades of grass and I think of this, and you
and the porch light in your hair, DeepWoods Off! on your skin,

the bareness of your right wrist. I wind in mackerel hooks
for the day. Go to the bathroom at the harbour,
an anchor on its sign. *MEN*. The bivalve shell: *WOMEN*.
Run water from a Waltec faucet. Pump soap. Scrub off
blood, scales. Count the money I've yet to be paid.

29

Clouds busy, sky mercurial as the tide
beneath my feet. Sheet of rain heading
east over sea wanting to scald. The order given:
Pack her in quick, boy. Get to moving.

A fast steam in this new-to-Dad boat,
what he got instead of giving me a raise.
I told you this: coppering the keel in the yard,
its blue floors and shit transmissions, and now

the paint peels to reveal rotten plywood, and lightning
surges over my island. Caught in a downpour
as I tie up. Rain and hail coming on like fresh grief,
funeral weather. All this happens so I can tell you

I love you. That someday we will look at the weather
out the same pane, or be out with your son
among the puddles, the tapping of rain.

30

I show you this poem as it's being wrote,
trying to take shape, a rickety frame raised
from this wave-rocked cradle, from mackerel blood.
You tell me you think it's good, *but*
you speak in absences. So it would be
Home is a place the door is never closed.

Closed is too soft a word for this house,
where I grew up, where a bat got took to a bedroom
door for a young Will not wanting to work.
And young Tom in the bathroom. My father roaring.
That door never locked my whole life.

Where my father took our old cat, the one he named Angus,
and shot it out back behind lobster traps stacked
the summer I was 16 and hadn't yet learned to be mean,
my hands softer than sunsets, more tender than morning.

You know what work is. We talked about this
before: an act of love. What puts food on the table,
electricity in the filaments. Go, turn a tap.
Does water fill the sink? Open the breadbox,
see the bag of flour. What else could work be?

RAISE FOUR WALLS
AND BE GRATEFUL

BAD HEARTS ON THE GO

Your father at the electric kettle on the counter,
weight on his palms watching snow
out the west window with its north-wind slant.
He lets you know about the bad hearts on the go:

This man might be forty-five and he's hospital-bound.
This other fella lived to be seventy-one, bragged
about lasting a year longer than his brother,
till he dropped his daughter off at the airport

and fell dead on his way out the door. A schoolteacher
on the ice, your cousin's husband in the shower.
Buddy up the road told by the moonshine-brewing
doctor half his heart don't work like it should.

Your father talks in warning, his own worries. The catch
with bad habits is they catch up. The kettle clicks off.
He pours water in his cup, says to you,
That's how it goes. You don't know when. Just. Bang.

You say, *Do something with flowers*,
when I sign your book, but I don't know flowers.
What is known: a bluefin tuna has scales
the size of loonies. Nor'west wind off the Gulf
brings whatever weather it wants. Out our window
sunlight fills glass buildings, and in the square
people skate. Earlier you made coffee, said,
You know, it really gets me going.

You got wrote about before, but not properly.
In pages somewhere you chop carrots,
shout from the can. *But it's not really me.*
I think it would be a neat trick to capture
a facet to pass off as whole. You say
you never thought you could be loved—you catch
yourself on this word, replace it with *care.*
I never thought I could be cared for.

What I want is a way to talk about all this, describe
how the bedsheet wraps around you, the look
over your shoulder when you catch on this word,
love. To say this is the bloom of hemlock
that needs cutting, show you squared teeth
of a bandsaw blade that needs replacing,
its baring wore with no support for the motor.

COUPLES' DINNER IN HAMILTON

We're going, you say, half-forget your coat, stumble
over our hosts' winter boots. Heels hammer
wooden stairs like false washboards
gone on or tore off. The parking lot
where we stop to look up: the pair of them slow
to shut their door, but it does close. I say,
What happened? Are you alright?
I was trapped with the man, enduring talk of sci-fi
and city cycling while you helped with the dishes.
The woman took your hair, held it.
Like this, you say, fingers gripping imaginary leader,
looking for nicks, forerunners of a snap under tension.
And she said, 'You're so beautiful.
Does Chris appreciate you?
Are you appreciated?'
Our car waits across the street by graveyard gates.
Moonlight breaks, momentary, a prodding nibble
on a tuna line before the smash, the dropping of red kite
held in sunlight by a helium balloon, before the fight
and you hold tight, not wanting for once to let go.

BARS AND FUNERALS

The bartender says her grandfather died, the pair
of you alone, and in the past you thought, *What if,*
but this moment is not tender. It is a relay of fact.
A forecast for the trip out, hours away with her PI
brother who spends days pursuing adulterers
living lives she says are *less exciting than you think.*

Sleet slides against windows of this lowlit
joint with its candles meant to be held close to lips
and blown out like shrapnel shavings from a pilot hole
before the lock finds the door. *You having one more?*

You want to tell her of your first funeral, old Gus.
Or how, when Jordan died at eleven, St. Columba
stogged full. Your school bus's slow roll past
the scene: the body bag's gleam surrounded by people
scattered along broken road holding each other
against the warm September sun.

HEAVY SEA

Late May and you stand in this yard like the memory
of your father when you were a boy. His garden first
started in egg cartons kept in the south building
with a fire fuelled by softwood. Something to keep him
in rhythm with the seasons. The morning after he was told,

he said to your mother, *It wasn't an easy life,*
but it was a good one, wasn't it?
The pair of them up all night with what the doctor
printed on paper, the finality of flesh turned word,
spread formalized to *metastasized*, a loose door rattled

between draught and doorframe. No space for dream
between head and pillow. She said, *Yes*, repeating herself
from St. Columba's front steps the year before Peter was born,
that name you share with a bit of your blood like biscuits
at Christmas dinner. The years between then and now ask,

Did any of this happen? To live is to do without clear answer.
Memory is made and remade each morning like sunlight
or shoreline. The Gulf tormented by a gale, its reckless violence
in 1851 wracked the Island with wrecks and dead bodies,
ships drove from their anchors, hands lost under brass sky,

swallowed by heavy sea. Your father with his own, Souris Hospital.
Morphine machines and slackened hands. Gus asking for whisky
once more, and then a puff of air, and gone. Your father saying,
He never stopped drinking till they put the tag on his toe.
What he says at the table you're meant to keep to yourself.

You scour this square for whatever you kept inside, here,
where you worked cooked lobster shells into red earth,
the topsoil turned by the tractor's tiller. Where your father
drove in hockey sticks for stakes, made the plastic wrap
from bait blocks into shelter when hard rains fell.

PROOF OF LIFE

Death is certain, she says,
handing you the small teacup.
That's why I see something, someone I want
to talk to, I just go for it, man.

Liszt plays on piano his "Years of Pilgrimage."
Images flash past on her computer screen:
her father's ashes on microscope slides spliced
with space pictures, starscapes, nebulae,
these lights you only seen spiked too far above
to know, truly, or broken in ocean before
the boat's bow, bled pale and white in the wake
of what makes up your survival.

This will prove there is life,
something   after death.

She steps from the counter, smooth movement
of her flowing in front of blinds that block
mountains, scant falling snow, the oil-painting sky.
Liszt goes on, playing to his countess sometime
in 1838, and now, and at the lake your father sits, waits
for the confirmation call: cancer, the body letting go.

Her voice pulls you from this when she says,
How is your tea?

                    Fine, you say. *About fit to make me believe.*

YOU'RE ALWAYS LEAVING

She says this, and it's true:
leaving the Island, that cradle
that once held you as a father
holds his child's dog, seizing
its way to death, teeth-breaking panic
and all piss and shit, and you're always

leaving Ontario: the mainland and promised
new beginning with its cheaper bread
and same-priced potatoes and the place
you rent whose rooms are clear-sky blank,
where she walked and placed her palm
against hodgepodge walls, talked curtains
and paintings to go up, books she'd read.

Transitory, transient, split like a loose mackerel
against a bandsaw blade. All your clothes
fit in one duffle bag. An ex called you *Spartan*,
and at a bar named like the card pirates get to mark
them for death, in a city that never became anything
but another layout to forget, your woman says

You're always leaving
though you never want to go
and she don't seem to want to keep you.

LOVE LETTER WRITTEN IN A PEI SPRING

This place is cut from a Ray Carver collection:
woodsmoke-coloured clouds, sun without warmth.
Even the red fields pale in what passes for spring.
Frost heaves in pavement, bare trees without buds.

You said to me, *Nature is resilient.* My Island proof
of this: by the time you touch down, summer
will be in swing. Lupins, dandelions. Singing sands
hot against your bare feet. Flowers bloom
by waterfront restaurants. I think of things to tell you.

Last night heavy rain. A man said of the weather:
It's a pile of wind we got. I don't know
when it'll get a chance to fine up.

And when I head to the mailbox here,
I think *hummingbird.* I think *summer.*
I think of the set of snowdrops you sketched
in a notebook where I wrote

She is someone you build a life with.
Put down foundation. Raise four walls
and be grateful.

TORONTO

She hates it here, but don't think she will
be here long. How she speaks to you
about leaving—to a northern wilderness
where she can form stories in moonglow
hook-sharp and clear as knifemarks in bark,
or to the east across the Atlantic to find
whatever history her family's kept
horizon-far and opaque. This wish she picks
as a herring scale from your hair, blows
away in hopes for it to come true. She looks
out the window of her high-rise apartment,
turns on the bedroom light to see herself
reflected in this city. She cannot let go.

SUFFERING

Friday evening and over the eastern hill
the moon, low and orange like a fire
your father would call *suffering* same as a drink
if it lasts longer than ten minutes.
What he said of his mother's final days
in Souris' Dying Room, her mind good but the body
letting her down, and her dying that suffering's end.
A kitchen table proclamation from Elmira's north edge.
Maybe it's best to learn the hard things young
and never forget. You ask yourself what you're doing
here alone with nothing but the smell of fallen apples
that can't cover autumn fields, their cowshit spread.

ONLY REPLACEMENT WILL DO

I

Rodney's poplars bend to meet the road, while
on the radio, a man in South Rustico says
every year the storms get worse. Every year,
a storm like this. *There's only so many trees.*
My uncle on Timber Lane Road, he only has five trees left!

The broadcaster says, *Are you an Islander?*

                    I mean, are you from *the Island?*

II

Last night wind hummed through the house,
the house a thrumming low-toned tuning fork.
To be inside an upstairs bedroom was to be inside
the heartbeat of a nervous heart seeking departure
from a chest that it never should have let take hold.

III

Evergreens along the yard's south side show their roots.
So many trees beat apart, the air smells like the woods
when you were a child with your father, and the saw
going. Then, you packed wood onto the truck wagon,
off-loaded through the basement hatch as sparse snow
spiraled around your 5-year-old body. A stick shaped
like a rifle your father let you keep as a gift for helping.
Now: Broken branches hold house siding.
The roof has shingled the yard.

IV

Ryan's building at the lake has caved in.
All what holds it is the traps it held,
packed to the studs, stacked clear to the rafters.
Seawater to Tom's knee on Red Bank Road.
Him in shorts, his old sneakers, to pump out
the *Sybil C.*, towels off in the car and curses
your father over speaker phone without
knowing. The rush and danger to driving
causes a fuck-up in hanging up and
your father is hurt. Powerlines whip the wind.
South of North Lake fish plant, a house gave up
its roof to the field. Gannets stand dying
in the flooded parking lots of harbours,
such a hard year for birds.

V

Will curses Rodney's cottonwood, *the cocksucking*
fucking things, those *shitty fucking poplars*
that should be *fucking banned* with their mess
of widespread roots kept shallow by nature.
This flimsy excuse for geotropism takes no hold
when a hard gale blows. At Will's, the trees roar:
wind, ocean sounds, blood trembling in
an ear when a conch's shell is pressed too tight.

VI

Phone connections drop in real life
and on the radio. You cannot reach family
that owns you how one owns a flashlight
that's hard to find when the dark barges in,
the family you seldom hold. What you gather:
> Cape Breton one of the worst hit, though
> you missed the first bit of broadcast.
> A voice through the speaker says,
> *The landscape of PEI has changed.*

VII

The wind is gone from a hum to the whine you know
from winter, the sort your father says will fill graveyards,
carry away the sick and unsuspecting, like the starling
you see try to leave twisted tree limbs across the road.
Its wings work their small muscles, gift locomotion to hollow
bones, but a gust rips through like the tide when a moon's on.

It's 5:26 before the sky clears to the west'ard, and the sun
tries to shine before it sinks into shattered treeline.
A woman from Port aux Basques says
the road by hers is washing away. The side wall buckles.
Buoys, pieces of buildings, float. A mile marker
is in her bay, unhooked from its mooring. She says,

My house has her dancing shoes on
and she's doing the hoochie coochie.

She prays tonight's high tide won't do away with more.
Waits for the weatherman's words to come true.
People are missing, a woman. One pulled from the ocean.

There's streets missing, old houses gone.
Where there was neighbourhoods, there's devastation.

VIII

In Shediac, people venture out to fetch fuel for generators.
The Stanhope golf course clubhouse caught in a flood,
before catching fire, reduced itself to ash and memories
in that certain sort of man with more money than you
will have to spend, who walk manicured grass, talk finance
and Fox News and bitch about, possibly with some approximation
of love, their housewives at home, who themselves sit with wine
in their hands and lonely hearts locked in chests filled only
with wind, the refuse left by a tide finding its way out.

Nine days in, and those with hope in the province,
faith in the Red Cross, start to see that forecast
looks pretty fucking bleak, and so seek resilience
in sleek new machines made for this
throwaway world, not our slightly used lives.
They fire up their fresh-got Champion generators
bought with cash from flat wallets and filled with gas
got waiting hours, on foot, in line in Stratford.
CBC tells of broke telephone poles, high-voltage
on the road. Do not drive over or under downed powerlines.
Do not touch trees that touch them. Do not blame those who failed
for their preventable and predictable failures. Thank them
for taking from the money you make pulling and dragging
your littoral life away, and spinning it into roundabout pavement,
new rinks, their own raises, as they tell you, *Tighten your belts*.
As they say, *Be patient*, as they say, *Be kind*.

X

Now: the starlings start
in their small clusters, almost
succeed. Neighbours go get
their chainsaws going, and give up.
Once down, the trees will stay put.

Morell wharf partly washed away, concrete
barriers shuffled like chess pieces.
Harbours everywhere fixed *good enough*
through the years are busted lobster traps
on rock bottom in a rough sea, beat to pieces
so badly only replacement will do.

XII

There is an intimacy to people provinces apart
stationed around small radios, tuned
to the same station seeking comfort, some small lift
with the load they're loaded with. We listen:

A reporter hesitates trying to place a town
on the western or eastern part of PEI's northside.
A retired firefighter walks his dog, Bella,

and this man, he tells us the sun is shining, this man,
he lets us know the air is clear and the sky cloudless,
this man, he says, *Today is a day to count your blessings.*

She practices fiddle near the open upstairs window.
The black and white TV glow goes with her notes

out to you, down in the driveway in need of salt.
You eat fresh snow from a gloved hand. Listen to her,

the creak of ice-rinded power lines, traffic's tuneless hum
thrumming toward town. Scrape of plough blades. Far away

from her father's slow death, the wasting. Tap water she put
to his lips that he spit out, saying, *You got anything stronger*

than that shit? There was talk of life then as though it flickered
past, a tall-ship apparition in thick mist lifting off the Strait.

Do you remember after? When she told you? Window open,
saying, *Sit.* Talking in future tense. Snow falling lightly.

EARLY DECEMBER

I read a story about a boy diagnosed with death,
meant to live with his death in his mother's house
as he grows to adulthood. He takes to rot,
feels the nothing creep in. There is a meaning to this
I can't parse, so, to Carver:
                                    two best friends
married and unhappy with their lives, and drink
themselves drunk, pursue two young girls to a cliff.
Lake water mirrors the darkness in one man
using a stone each for the girls. A menacing end.

A city writer said to me, *Carver's problem was*
he was bored all the time. Out the south kitchen window,
trees are stripped of leaves, the land of trees.
Through what's left: battered barn roof, a sky
that wants to rain. There are worse ways to spend
a December morning, and I will have done
them all by the end of my life.

ACKNOWLEDGEMENTS

Thanks to my folks, first and foremost. They brought me into the world even though I never asked them to, but now that I been around for a bit I can't imagine being anywhere else. And though I can't speak for my siblings, for whom my parents did the same, I will thank them for their general endurance of my endeavors.

A big thank you to Kyle and Bianca Gallant, Brendan Shepherd, Steve McOrmond, Will and Bre Alexander, Dave Hickey, Keith Burgoyne, Evie Christie, Amber McMillan, Walker MacDonald, Kevin Delaney, Jamie Tennant, Rachel Leslie, Owain Nicholson, Victoria Hetherington, Stuart Ross, Annick MacAskill, Tony Sciara, Jill Blanchard, A.W. French, Terry Hawes, and Jake Skakun. All of you have read at least some of these poems along the way / generally put up with me carrying on about anything from a book I read to a sore shoulder to the weather to something done on a lobster boat or in a grocery store with more patience than you should've.

A special thanks to Shane Pendergast, and his family, and the Jack Pine Folk Club. You've given a space and gentle spectacle to local poets and musicians in a province that needs it, and that's an importance that should be underlined.

Thank you to the North Writers Group members: Greg Rhyno, Aaron Tang, Ashish Seth, Simone Dalton, John Currie, Walt Palmer, and Kris Bone. Our conversations have been propulsive and generative, and aided in this book's revisions.

I'm indebted to those who guided me from the jump to now: Deirdre Kessler, Richard Lemm, Lorna Crozier, Dionne Brand, Elizabeth Philips, Catherine Bush, and Michael Winter. All of you have seen the value in my writing, even when I felt I'd be better off being an accountant. If it weren't for Dionne suggesting I submit to McClelland & Stewart, this book might still be searching for a home. Her generosity and patience with me is something I'm very grateful for.

I can't thank Canisia Lubrin and Kelly Joseph enough. Seriously. I can't come up with a follow up line. So thank you for everything along the journey with this book. It's been great.

There are facts in this book that aren't true. This is due to my mistaking them as true at the time of writing or believing the falsehoods sound better than the alternative. If you can't tell the difference, my job's done.

Matt Lieb, half-quoted in "We Talked About This" is, with Vince Mancini, a host of *The Frotcast*, a movie podcast where the phrase "mamma's mean juice" came from. I been listening to that podcast since it started, and love it, even if they hate art.

Versions of "Cutting Bait" and "This Word" appeared in *The Fiddlehead* 285.

A version of "The Heart Is a Knot" appeared in *Watch Your Head: Writers and Artists Respond to the Climate Crisis* (Coach House Books, 2020).

A version of "Dirt" appeared in *The Antigonish Review* 204.

"All This Is" was published as a poetry pamphlet by Annick MacAskill through her wonderful Opaat Press.

"Love Letter Written in a PEI Spring" was published in *The BUZZ*'s August 2024 edition. A thank you to Bren Simmers for this.

The father's ending quote in "All This Is" might be recognized from my essay "Nothing But Water," found in *Brick* 102. It's something my father said to me and the truth behind it has plagued me since. Hopefully you are similarly infected.

CHRIS BAILEY is a graphic designer and commercial fisherman from Prince Edward Island. He holds a MFA in Creative Writing from the University of Guelph. Chris' writing has appeared in *Grain, Brick, The Fiddlehead, Best Canadian Stories 2021, Best Canadian Stories 2025,* and elsewhere. His debut poetry collection, *What Your Hands Have Done,* is available from Nightwood Editions. His piece *Fisherman's Repose* was a winner of the 2022 BMO 1st Art! Award. *Forecast: Pretty Bleak* is his second poetry collection.